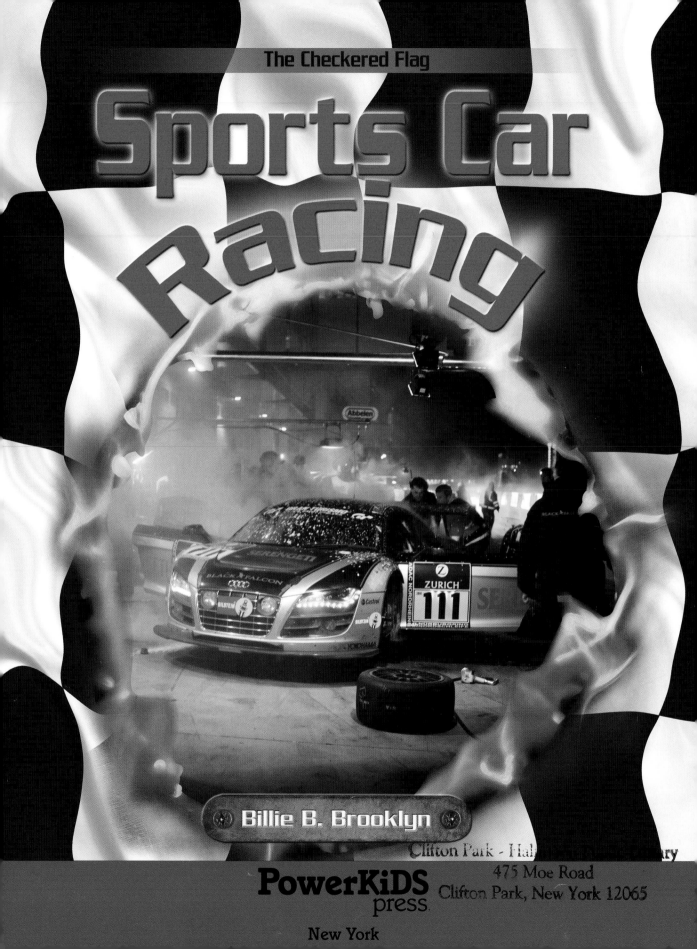

The Checkered Flag

Sports Car Racing

Billie B. Brooklyn

PowerKiDS press.

New York

Clifton Park - Halfmoon Public Library
475 Moe Road
Clifton Park, New York 12065

Published in 2015 by **The Rosen Publishing Group, Inc.**
29 East 21st Street, New York, NY 10010

Library of Congress Cataloging-in-Publication-Data
Brooklyn, Billie. Sports car racing / Billie Brooklyn.
   pages cm. — (Checkered Flag)
 Includes index.
ISBN 978-1-4994-0166-0 (pbk.)
ISBN 978-1-4994-0136-3 (6 pack)
ISBN 978-1-4994-0160-8 (library binding)
1. Sports car racing—Juvenile literature. 2. Grand Prix racing—Juvenile literature. I. Title.
 GV1029.13.B76 2015
 796.72—dc23
                                              2014033943

6817

Developed and produced for Rosen by BlueAppleWorks Inc.
Art Director: T. J. Choleva
Managing Editor for BlueAppleWorks: Melissa McClellan
Designer: Joshua Avramson
Photo Research: Jane Reid
Editor: Joanne Randolph

Photo Credits: cover, p. 16–17 bottom, 18 bottom, 23 right, 25 Walter Arce/Dreamstime; title page Sebastian Wahsner/Dreamstime; TOC, p. 13, 16 right Oskar SCHULER/Shutterstock; p. 4 top SPYDERMAN360/Creative Commons; p. 4 bottom Steve Mann/Shutterstock; p. 4–5 bottom avarand/Shutterstock; p. 5 top Natursports/Dreamstime; p. 5 middle, 17 left Beelde Photography/Shutterstock; p. 6 top D.A.S. (Germany)/Public Domain; p. 6–7 bottom, 21 right THE KLEMANTASKI COLLECTION; p. 7 right Maurie Hill/Dreamstime; p. 8–9 Diegoq/Dreamstime; p. 8 left, 8 right CHEN WS/Shutterstock; p. 9 right MatthiasKabel/Creative Commons; p. 10 top Creative Commons; p. 10 bottom Smokeonthewater/Creative Commons; p. 11 top Jeffrey Keeton/Creative Commons; p. 11 bottom Kobby Dagan/Shutterstock; p. 12 Julia Bauer/Dreamstime; p. 14 RUI FERREIRA/Shutterstock; p. 15 James Menges/Dreamstime; p. 16 top, 24 top Action Sports Photography/Shutterstock; p. 17 right, 18 top AMA/Shutterstock; p. 20 top Wonker/Creative Commons; p. 20–21 James Moy/Keystone Press; p. 22–23 Panoramic/Keystone Press; p. 25 right NL-HaNA, ANEFO/Creative Commons; p. 26 left Carlos Caetano/Shutterstock; p. 26–27 bottom Svetlana Day/Dreamstime; p. 27 top Sebastian Wahsner/Dreamstime; p. 28 Adam Tinney/Shutterstock

Manufactured in the United States of America

CPSIA Compliance Information: Batch #CW15PK: For Further Information contact: Rosen Publishing, New York, New York at 1-800-237-9932

Table of Contents

What Is Sports Car Racing?

Sports car racing uses cars that blend the features of racing cars, such as **Formula 1**, and touring cars, or cars that families might own.

Sports car racing is all about the exciting potential of the car. **Endurance**, reliability, and strategy are just as important as speed. Sports car racing is generally a team sport, especially for long races. During these long races, there are many drivers and regular driver changes. There are three main types of sports cars for racing:

- Grand Touring (GT) models based on high performance sports cars available for sale to the public
- Prototypes built just for racing
- Touring (ST) models based upon smaller or family cars such as hatchbacks or sedans

Sports prototypes are one-of-a-kind machines that bear no relation to any road vehicles.

Touring sports car races feature heavily modified street or family cars.

Two Seaters

Sports car racing is not to be confused with Formula 1 and **NASCAR**, two other major motorsports. Most sports cars have two seats, though some have four, and the wheels are closed in. Sports cars are manufactured all over the world, by companies such as Porsche, Bugatti, Audi, Aston Martin, Ford and other high-performance car manufacturers.

Formula 1 cars have their wheels outside the body of the car.

NASCAR car wheels are closed in, but there's only one seat (the driver's seat).

A Porsche 997 GT makes a spectacular jump during a race. GT category is dominated by the world's top sports car brands.

History of Sports Car Racing

Sports car racing really got rolling with the 24 Hours of Le Mans in France in 1923. This race was about endurance rather than pure speed. The challenge was to see who could drive the greatest distance on a circuit or racecourse in a 24-hour period. There were other sports car races held before this, but Le Mans set the gold standard for testing the mechanical endurance of the cars.

The 24 Hours of Le Mans is the world's oldest active sports car race in endurance racing. The first race was held in 1923.

Sports car racing has been popular in Europe since the very first days of car racing.

Arrival in America

Sports car racing has always been very popular in Europe, but it took a little while longer to catch on in the U.S. There were no real professional sports car races in the United States until 1958. The arrival of new cars like the Ferrari GTO and Corvette increased the popularity of sports car racing in the 1960s, and in the late '60s the Ford GTO dominated at Le Mans.

The Can-Am race series was very popular in Canada and the United States from 1966 to 1987. McLaren-designed race cars reigned at these races with their reliability and innovative designs.

The 1979 McLaren M1B 5.3liter Can-Am race car competing in a Historics Revival Series.

Grand Touring Sports Cars

Designed for long, high-speed drives, luxury Grand Touring cars were adapted for racing early on. The modified models of the original street versions can attain impressive speeds and maintain the endurance required for longer circuit races.

Early models of Italian GT cars from manufacturers Alfa Romeo, Ferrari, and Lancia led the way in the 1920s. Corvettes, Aston Martins, and Porsches have all enjoyed wins in the GT racing class. Some of the modifications the cars undergo include wider tires, bigger brakes, better **aerodynamics**, and the use of more exotic construction materials.

Grand Touring racing is the most common form of sports car racing.

The Porsche 911 is currently one of the most popular cars in the GT class.

GRAND TOURING – GT

The term Grand Touring comes from the Italian language. *Gran turismo* refers to a grand tour or long, demanding drive across the country. It is applied to luxury cars able to make long-distance journeys, or grand tours, at higher speeds in comfort and style.

Unlike most race cars, which are built entirely for speed, grand tourers are also built for comfort and handling. Most GTs have engines in the front and rear-wheel drive. This creates more space for the cabin.

The Alfa Romeo 6C 1750 Gran Turismo Compressore 1932 model is a luxury automobile capable of high speed and long-distance.

Prototype Sports Cars

After decades of racing, prototype race cars became the ultimate sports cars in the 1960s. Prototypes can drive at speeds of more than 200 miles per hour (322 km/h). Designed exclusively to compete and win, prototype sports cars are not street legal. That means that they are not for purchase by the everyday consumer. **Purpose-built** for racing, they are too fast and too loud for use on regular roads.

The Corvette Daytona Prototype, released in 2012, marks the first prototype car Chevrolet had fully built in many years.

Sports prototypes (along with Formula 1 cars) introduce the newest technology and ideas to motorsport.

Built for Racing

Cars of this type are built to technical specifications set by specific races. Compared to **production-based** cars, these racers are allowed more flexibility within set race parameters. For example, a Le Mans Prototype 1 (LMP1) sports racer can have any number of engine cylinders, must weigh a minimum of 1,984 pounds (900 kilograms) and its fuel tank size is determined by the type of fuel it uses. Introduced in 2003, a Daytona Prototype racer uses 100 octane unleaded gasoline only and since 2014 has a six-speed transmission.

Milka Duno was the first woman to drive a Daytona Prototype.

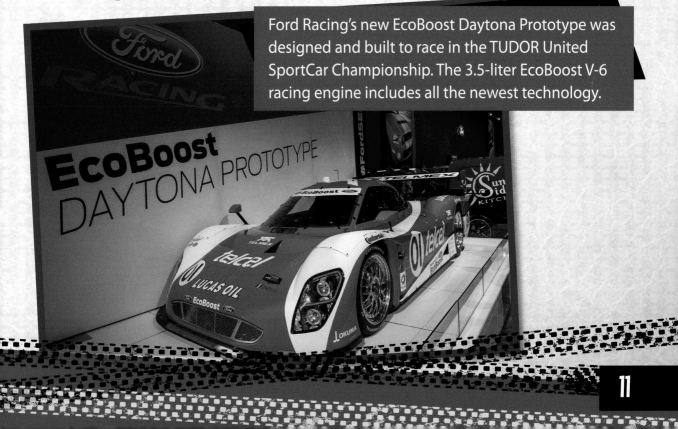

Ford Racing's new EcoBoost Daytona Prototype was designed and built to race in the TUDOR United SportCar Championship. The 3.5-liter EcoBoost V-6 racing engine includes all the newest technology.

Endurance Races

Endurance races are where sports car racing really tests the durability and performance of the car itself beyond the race team's driving skill and stamina. Whether for 24-hour events like Le Mans, for 12 Hours at Sebring, or "just" 10 hours at Petit Le Mans, the vehicle must be able to rise to the challenge.

⚠ **FAST FACT**

Drivers and vehicles in endurance races often win by a surprisingly narrow margin in spite of the long hours and great distances covered.

There are numerous categories and subcategories in endurance racing. Car type, manufacturer or private maker, the number of drivers on the team, the course, and event length all determine these categories. An example of a main category is Le Mans Prototype. A subcategory would be the difference between a Le Mans Prototype 1 (LMP1) and a Le Mans Prototype 2 (LMP2).

Most endurance races last from six up to 24 hours.

Tough on Drivers

Longer endurance races generally have teams with many drivers, who change often. Endurance race drivers must vary the way they drive in order to balance performance and fuel consumption. Longer races involve complex pit strategy to keep the cars going in the best possible shape. Drivers must also take into account such things as weight distribution and balance shifts in the car. Some of the most important technical advancements in motorsport racing have come of the extreme demands placed on car, track, driver, and crew in endurance races.

A team of drivers is required for endurance races to keep them alert during races.

Sprint Races

Sprint races are the shortest form of endurance race, lasting under 3 hours. There are one to three drivers per race team. The racetracks are oval or circular, and paved or made of dirt.

Sprint races often feature touring car races. Touring cars are heavily modified street cars. It can be hard to tell the difference between touring cars or "grand" touring sports cars (also known as GT cars). Touring cars are usually based upon family cars and have similar engines, while GT racing cars are based upon more powerful and more expensive sports cars, such as Ferraris or Porsches, and have modified engines.

Touring car races are popular all over the world, but even more so in Europe.

The IMSA Continental Tire Sports Car Challenge

The **IMSA** Continental Tire Sports Car Challenge is a grand touring and touring car racing series that also features sprint races. The traditional sports car racing format often runs both Grand Sport (GS) and a touring car based Street Tuner (ST) class on the same track at the same time. This is called a "combined" race, and there are two drivers per car. Sometimes the races will be run in "split classes," with separate races for both classes. This is especially common for shorter race venues.

While both are fun to race, the main difference between GS and ST cars is their engine power. The GS cars have very powerful engines that range from 8 to 12 cylinders. The ST cars are more like racing your own car, with engines ranging from 4 to 6 cylinders. Usually, the more cylinders an engine has, the more powerful it is.

The IMSA Continental Tire Sports Car Challenge races last 2.5 hours and require a change of drivers.

Sports Car Safety

Racing teams and race organizers work together to make sure that drivers stay safe during a race. They do this in many ways.

The driver is harnessed inside the car to keep from being ejected from the vehicle if an accident happens. Drivers also wear helmets and full-body fireproof suits. The HANS (Head and Neck Support) system is a special device that protects a driver's head and neck. It sits on top of the shoulders, behind the helmet.

Sports cars drivers are strapped into their car's cockpit by a strong harness.

Fireproof suits shield drivers from a fire until the rescue crews arrive.

Keeping Cool

Another risk for drivers inside the car is dehydration. The protective equipment worn is hot and made up of many layers, leading to extreme sweating. It is important for the driver to stay hydrated and cooled down, otherwise there is a risk of passing out while operating the car at a super high speed. Drivers drink through hoses with bite valves, and they usually stick to good old-fashioned water.

A SAFE COURSE

The racecourse itself is designed to be as safe as possible. Run-off areas in likely crash areas allow drivers to leave the course in a safe manner. They are also known as gravel traps. Air fences are positioned along these run-off areas, too, and act like already-open air bags. Medical and firefighting personnel are always on site and ready to respond at races.

Run-off areas are spaces off the track put aside for vehicles to leave the track safely in case of emergency.

The **HANS device** is a safety item required in many car racing sports.

Sports Car Racing Series

The **FIA** World Endurance Championship is made up of eight endurance races taking place around the world, including the 24 Hours of Le Mans race. The races have four different classes of race cars on the same track at the same time. There are LMP1 and LMP2 categories with sports prototypes competing in the Le Mans Prototype categories and the production-based grand tourers competing in GTE (E for Endurance) category. The GTE is divided into GTE Pro for teams with professional drivers, and GTE Am for mixed teams of amateur drivers.

World championship titles are awarded to the top scoring manufacturers and drivers over the season.

The first season of the TUDOR United SportCar Championship, 2014 featured 12 races held across North America.

American Favorites

⚠ **FAST FACT**

Riders without factory sponsorship are called **privateers**. With limited sponsorship, they must often buy their own equipment and pay their own race fees and travel costs.

The Pirelli World Challenge

The Pirelli World Challenge has been around for 25 years and evolved from the establishment of a street stock automobile classification. It is a North American series with five classes of vehicles: GT (Grand Touring), GTS (Grand Touring Sport), TC (Touring Car), and Touring Car A-Spec and B-Spec. B-Specs include smaller cars such as Mini Coopers and Nissan Versas, among others. A new class for amateur drivers, the GT-A class, began competing in 2014. There are up to 12 event weekends in a season and 14–16 races or rounds per event.

The TUDOR United SportCar Championship

The TUDOR United SportCar Championship is the product of a merger between the American Le Mans Series (ALMS) and the Rolex Sports Car Series. In January 2014, this series had its first race, beginning its season in Florida with the Rolex 24 Hours at Daytona. The Championship is now the premiere North American sports car racing series. There are four unique classes in the United SportCar Championship series: Prototype (P), Prototype Challenge (PC), GT Le Mans (GTLM), and GT Daytona (GTD).

24 Hours of Le Mans

Known as the "Grand Prix of Endurance and Efficiency," Le Mans is the oldest and most respected endurance race in the world. Begun in 1923 in France, it is a 24-hour race in which multiple classes of vehicles compete side-by-side. Teams compete for prizes within their own classes as well

The start of the 24 Hours of Le Mans is exciting for drivers and the fans alike.

as for the title of overall race winner. Drivers are behind the wheel for upwards of 2 hours (sometimes longer!) and teams are made up of a minimum of three drivers. Unlike races focused on speed, this one is all about the endurance and reliability of the car, which takes a beating after a 24-hour drive.

Audi Sport Team wins the 24 Hours of Le Mans race in 2014.

The Circuit

The track itself, 8.47 miles (13.6 km) in length, is called the Circuit de la Sarthe. It is made up of public roads (closed for the race) and permanent tracks. Over the years it has been modified to increase safety, with the addition of two **chicanes** to reduce the stretches of straight road where speeds once reached a dangerous 252 mph (405 km/h). The course no longer passes through the town of Le Mans as an additional precaution to protect spectators.

The Mercedes 300SLR of Pierre Levegh smolders on top of the embankment opposite the pits, having been completely consumed by fire in the greatest motor racing tragedy of all time.

21

Rolex 24 at Daytona

Formerly known as 24 Hours of Daytona, the Rolex 24 at Daytona is a 24-hour race held at Daytona International Speedway in Daytona Beach, Florida. Held in the off-season, it is known for attracting all-star drivers.

In 2002 a new set of rules was introduced regarding the kinds of cars that would be allowed to race at Daytona. In order to make sports car racing less expensive, the new cars, called Daytona Prototypes (DPs) would be built using cheaper materials and technology. The DPs began racing in 2003. No other kinds of cars were admitted to the race.

The 52nd running of the Rolex 24 in 2014 was the inaugural race for the TUDOR United SportCar Championship as well as the newly merged IMSA. As part of the new series, Le Mans Prototype and Le Mans GTE cars could participate for the first time in over a decade.

Giant Track

The track is 3.56 miles (5.7 km) long and is called a combined road course. A combined course is an oval track that features a road course in the **infield** that is linked to the oval circuit. At Daytona, the track is a tri-oval shape, which resembles an isosceles triangle. The back straightaway is interrupted with a chicane and the infield section includes two hairpin turns. Fifteen Florida sports stadiums could fit inside the Daytona International Speedway. That's big!

Rolex 24 at Daytona race in 2014 was the first race of newly formed TUDOR United SportCar Championship.

"STAR" DRIVERS

Hollywood movie stars sure seem to love racing cars. Since the beginning of racing history, famous actors have been hooked on testing their skill behind the wheel. Patrick Dempsey is an American race car driver you might recognize from the TV show *Grey's Anatomy* and the Transformers movie, *Dark of the Moon*. He has competed at 24 Hours of Daytona, 24 Hours of Le Mans, and the Baja 1000 Off-Road Race.

Actor Patrick Dempsey is part of a three-driver team called Dempsey Racing based out of Georgia.

12 Hours of Sebring

For over sixty years, some of the world's best drivers and manufacturers have competed in the 12 Hours of Sebring, an endurance race in Florida. Sebring is America's oldest road racing track and is on the former site of a military air base where B17 bombers were stationed. The first race was in 1952 and it continues annually, second only to Le Mans in prestige and popularity. It features many of the same cars and drivers from the Le Mans races.

The 12 Hours of Sebring is one of the most demanding endurance races.

Because the 3.7-mile (5.95 km) track is partly made of pavement and partly of concrete (laid out in the 1940s when the track was a military airfield), and because it experiences dramatic surface changes with the rising Florida temperatures, it makes for some super tough and bumpy driving conditions. Described by more than one driver as "**grueling**," it is also said that 12 Hours of Sebring is even more demanding than some 24-hour races.

The 12 Hours of Sebring race is also one of three races in the informal Triple Crown of endurance racing.

TRIPLE CROWN

There are three jewels in the Triple Crown of endurance racing: 12 Hours of Sebring, 24 Hours of Le Mans, and the Rolex 24 at Daytona. All three races are serious challenges: imagine winning all three! Several endurance drivers have won this special crown, including A. J. Foyt, Hurley Haywood, Al Holbert, and Mauro Baldi, to name just a few. Many drivers have come close to winning with second-place finishes in the third event. These drivers include Ken Miles (denied a win at 24 Hours of Le Mans in 1966), Mario Andretti (Le Mans 1995), and Allan McNish (Daytona 2012).

Mauro Baldi is one of the few race car drivers to win the Triple Crown.

Meet the Pit Crew

Racing at high speeds is very tough on cars. Sports cars need to stop several times during a race for gas and fresh tires. It may look like racing a sports car is an individual sport, but it's not. No race car driver works alone. It takes a whole team to participate in winning a race.

Pit crew members need to be good at what they do and work fast.

The maintenance work is done by pit crew members. The pit crew is an important part of the race team. It can be made up of 4 to 20 mechanics and technicians, depending on race rules.

The pit box is a taped-off area in the pit row.

Action in the Pit

In sports car racing, the pit is where refueling and tire changing take place, along with minor repairs to the car. It's also where a change of drivers happens for different kinds of endurance racing. The period of time that a driver is at the wheel in a race with more than one driver is called his or her "**stint**."

At endurance races, pit crew members are ready to work through the night.

Pit stops are longer during endurance races because heavier demands on the car mean that more scheduled maintenance is required.

The driver must pull the car into the pit box and turn off the engine before the car can be serviced.

You and Sports Car Racing

If you love race cars and want to see more of them, you can whet your appetite by watching races on TV or on YouTube, or in person at a track near you. There are lots of great movies and video games that feature race car driving, too.

One of the easiest ways to get a firsthand taste for racing is to drive go-karts. And if you're really excited to try out the thrill of racing, you might also want to check out something called Quarter Midget Racing. It's a competitive sport for kids age 5–16. This popular youth sport started in the 1930s in California and it has spread across North America like wildfire. Training programs that let you learn to drive and follow the rules before trying to compete are highly recommended by experts in the field.

You must "retire" from Quarter Midget racing by age 16, but most youth drivers have already moved on to bigger, faster cars, like full Midget racers, by then.

Sports Car Racing Flags

Green Flag
Start of practice, qualifying or race. Also used for race restart after caution (yellow flag) and red flag periods.

Red Flag
This flag means the race has been stopped. The cause is usually unsafe conditions brought on by bad weather or a bad accident.

Yellow Flag
There is a potentially hazardous situation; drivers slow down and keep their position.

Black Flag
This tells a driver to return to the pit. It is usually waved with a car number, and often indicates that a driver is being disqualified.

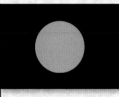

Black Flag with Orange Disk
Driver is to leave the track because of a mechanical problem. It is waved with a car number.

Yellow Flag with Red Stripes
This flag warns drivers when there is debris, fluid, or oil on the track.

Blue Flag
The driver is about to be overtaken by faster drivers and must yield to them.

Black and White Flag
Last warning before exclusion from the race for nonsporting driving.

Checkered Flag
Race is over. All drivers want to see the checkered flag waved at them first, as that means they have won!

Glossary

aerodynamics The study of forces and how they affect objects as they move through air.

chicane Artificially-created "S" turn in the track that is usually placed after long stretches of straight track to help control the speed of the racers.

endurance The ability to keep going for long periods of time under challenging conditions.

FIA Fédération Internationale de l'Automobile is the French name for the organization that controls auto racing.

Formula 1 A form of auto racing featuring open-wheel cars that follow a set "formula" for their construction. Also known as F1.

grueling Very tough, tiring conditions.

HANS device The Head and Neck Support (HANS) system is equipment used by drivers to help prevent injuries to these crucial areas.

IMSA The International Motor Sports Association.

infield The area inside the boundary of the track that often includes the garage area.

NASCAR The National Association for Stock Car Auto Racing, the leading organization for stock car racing in the world.

privateer Independent driver of race cars who competes alongside manufacturers.

production-based Cars modeled after cars created for purchase by the general public.

purpose-built Cars built for racing only.

stint The length of time a driver is behind the wheel during a race.

For More Information

Further Reading

Aloian, Molly. *Ferrari.* Crabtree Pub Co., 2010.

Doeden, Matt. *Sports Car Racing.* Lerner Publishing Group, 2009.

Dredge, Richard. *World's Fastest Cars: The Fastest Road and Racing Cars on Earth.* Haynes Publishing, 2011.

Websites

Due to the changing nature of Internet links, PowerKids Press has developed an online list of websites related to the subject of this book. This site is updated regularly. Please use this link to access the list: **www.powerkidslinks.com/tcf/spcar**

Index